DID28301

FINISHING LINE PRESS

www.finishinglinepress.com

All The Beauty

This is for Ken

ACKNOWLEDGMENTS

Appalachian Review: "Spring"
Atlanta Review: "I watch him, my husband"
Bellevue Literary Review: "Lost time," "Autobiography"
Burningword Literary Journal: "Rice Balls," "Playlist in June"
Chelsea Station Magazine: "Where I Come From"
Crosswinds Poetry Journal: "After AIDS," "London," "Fifty Minutes"
Dogwood: A Journal of Poetry and Prose: "Jocks"
The Florida Review: "The Dusk Effect"
Mason's Road: "Jocks"
Mudfish: "Birdbaths on Amazon," "After being vaccinated, second dose, at
Javits onvention Center, March 2021"
Ruminate Magazine: "Runaway Dorothy Was the Name of the Band"
Vallum Magazine: "Child Psychologist"

Many thanks are due to the Writers Studio community, which has given me
so much, especially my teachers, Philip Schultz and Lesley Dormen, and my
fellow Master Class students, both past and present, currently including, at
the time of this writing, Julianne Bond, Anne Chinnis, Nancy Conners, Stas
Gawronski, Judith Gerbin, Andrea Marcusa, Francesca Moroney, Wendell
Tong and Cindy Wheeler. Additional thanks to my friend and writing
companion, Kim Farrar.

Publisher: Leah Huete de Maines
Editor: Christen Kincaid
Cover Art: Margot Hardesty, *The Chair in Easton*
Author Photo: Ken Lustbader
Cover Design: Elizabeth Maines McCleavy

Order online: www.finishinglinepress.com
also available on amazon.com

Author inquiries and mail orders:
Finishing Line Press
PO Box 1626
Georgetown, Kentucky 40324
USA

Table of Contents

Remembering

Outside my kitchen window
it is a bright winter morning,
one where the rising light hovers
in clear radiant air
before quickly giving way to new light
and more of the day starts to happen
and I know that I am watching the earth spin
with bodies and ashes, forgotten and forsaken,
spinning with it, but still,
what does one do with all the beauty.

Rice Balls: New York, 1983

Your skin is yellow and you
weigh about 100 pounds.
Your face is gaunt and your
eyes bulge out of your head
like the eyes of fly. You are
inert, wasted and wasting.
You got the flu but it wouldn't go
away and then came the lesions,
first on your shoulder then your
chest and now they cover your
torso like you've been leeched in
the Dark Ages. You took yourself
to the ER where you lay on a
gurney in your own shit for hours
and then you were put in isolation,
told you have AIDS and now
you will never be touched by
an ungloved hand again.

And it keeps getting worse.
Your veins burn from one medicine
while your brain is being eaten
alive by some virus only birds get.
Meals are pushed into your room
by terrified orderlies but you
can't bear to eat them because the
lesions are in your throat too. Your life
has become some medieval nightmare
and apparently you are going to
expire in absolute agony.

It is the reverse trajectory of
The Wizard of Oz where you
are thrust backwards into a
grim black and white world
forever banished from the
vibrancy of your beloved
New York that you chose
like a promised land.

Only a month ago you were at
home in your 5th floor walk-up
with the slanted floors and
high ceilings in Little Italy
where a fat lady with big red
hair sat outside your window
at a card table selling rice balls
out of tin foil pans. She made
them in her tenement kitchen and
would show up every day at 3 yelling
Rice balls, come and get 'em!
just when the local school lets
out with the mostly Chinese kids
whose mothers were there to get them,
and no one was speaking English.
The rice ball lady had a broom the
handle of which she would wave
and poke at people, mostly Black
people, when she didn't like them.
Once you called the police to
report this and they just laughed
when you told them where
you lived.

And now, nothing is left of you but
this wasting, gasping, collapsing, fevered
body well on its way to becoming a
corpse. The doctor tells you, through
his surgical mask, that you are
"putting up a good fight" but you'd
like to hit him with the handle
of a broomstick and finally
buy one of those rice balls.

Spring

(In Memory of Martha)

One winter in the late afternoon
my aunt and I took a drive
out into the countryside
and watched as the sun began to set
over icy fallow farm fields
its shallow oblique light
the very thing she wanted me to see
because it was beautiful.
Aunts you see run in my family
even though I only had one
she came from a long line
of strong aunts
mountain women
who fended for themselves
even taking in other people's children
like she took me in once
when as a young man
I was waiting to die of AIDS
and the city had become a mortuary
so I had to get out.
One evening in early April
we stood outside listening
to chirping sounds
to peepers my aunt said
I didn't know what those were
baby frogs she told me.

Lost Time

It was on an airplane that I let my
Mother read the first paragraph of
Swann's Way, my travel reading.
She, the eternal English major,
Confessed that she'd never read
Proust. Her eyes were wide with
Delight as she said "now *that* is a
sentence!" the one about the
gentle boy grasping the ephemeral
mysteries and terrors of sleeping and
waking. Then somewhere over Virginia
I think, I had some reason to tell her
that almost all of my friends had
died of AIDS. She burst into tears,
putting her head in her hands,
stiff and bent from arthritis and
I realized that I had never told anyone
that fact before. As we parted at
LaGuardia, she to the suburbs
and I to the city, she looked at me, her
right eye red from a blood vessel that
burst when she cried, and said
"I had no idea" her voice almost a
whisper, her eyes again filling
with tears as she turned and
walked away, pulling her small,
compact suitcase behind her.

After AIDS

(In memory of Danny and Lee and David)

The weeds I found in my driveway
this morning
pulled up easily enough, although
I did have to
yank a bit on that clump of grass,
kneeling down, getting my fingers
below the gravel, close to the dirt so
I could pull and tug at the root, the rip
and tear of it so satisfying, the small
dark hole left behind
a testament to my devotion.

Every morning, every
walk with the dog,
I am constantly bending over to
pull up even the smallest
of weeds, or to pick up a stick
or remove a stray pinecone,
tossing them into the woods,
wiping the dirt from my fingers
and then smoothing out
the small stones.

In the winter, when it snows,
I resist getting the driveway plowed
worrying about how the heavy blade
will disturb the gravel,
displacing it, scattering it,
or how, if the snow is deep,
the plow guy won't quite see
the curves of the driveway
damaging the moss and periwinkle
that grow alongside it and I fear
that when the snow melts
my heart will break.

At the end of the driveway
is a witch hazel tree,
a tree that flowers in the winter,
small bright yellow blossoms
coat its thin branches appearing
usually in February
before spring, before forsythia
or crocuses or even snow drops,
before everything else,
but then again,
after it all, too.

Autobiography

I wrote a poem
about loneliness
called Hunger
where a young man
sees a hungry look
in my eyes
and at the end
I reveal that
as a child
I was rarely
touched
that I suffered
from a kind of
sensory deprivation
but what I left out
of this poem
was my body
now and how
I had sex
with the young man
who saw the look
in my eyes
he kept feeding
himself to me
and I loved it
or how I am
HIV positive
and have been
for nearly all
of my adult life
something I often
allude to but never
simply say

out of fear
but there it is
and so what you might think
no one dies of AIDS anymore
but the thing is
there is no me
there is no body
desired or desiring
no man quietly
remembering
a child's hunger
without the
steady presence
of a virus
and so I couldn't wait
to tell you these things
because without
this knowledge
you really don't
know me at all.

The Dusk Effect

To be seen in the correct light—
isn't this worth waiting for
even though the unvarnished, clear eyed,
bird's eye view is a near impossibility
like in the dim slant of the morning
when dust motes float out from under my bed
circling the air, faults big as field mice,
my mouth dry and tasting of yellowed plastic,
my mind still keening from sleep,
or in London at dusk when I find myself
standing on the exact same corner
I stood on at twenty and watch
as the present day suddenly fades away—
phone booth, post box, double-decker bus, bricks, even blood,
all these reds recede, swirling and congealing at my feet
leaving behind a blue veined line
of a life defined by a disease,
a life the boy on the corner never saw coming
and just as I think I am going to fall,
somewhere between the gasp and the near collapse,
sorrow emerges from the gloaming like a violet
for me to touch, hold close, and tend to.

London

If only you could've seen me that night
making my way home,
changing trains at Leicester Square,
knowing my way, gliding down
that long escalator, walking
past tourists and theater goers,
past boys with hair swept high
over their all-cheekbone faces,
and me, smiling, plain as day,
you would've stopped in your tracks
and said ah! Yes! *There* he is.
I didn't know this would happen
that evening at an art opening
in Earl's Court, didn't know
I would feel something like this,
some edition of myself
as if for the first time,
my pockets stuffed full of Pounds Sterling
and Google Maps,
my eyes blinking like the leaves
I see on the plane trees
that line this city's streets,
so tolerant of people and pollution,
my ears ringing only with the sound
of nothing being wrong
as I sipped red wine and conversed
with strangers, even smoking
a couple of cigarettes in the garden out back
under the amber cast of the London sky
that had been so good to me.

Where I Come From

What was it I wanted to say
at a dinner the other night when
someone asked me if I thought
that this bad thing that happened
to me wasn't really a *blessing
in disguise?* Such an annoying
phrase. As if the bad thing didn't
actually occur, didn't do real
damage. As if bad things were
mere delivery devices for
hidden blessings. In between
the nodding of my head and
well, yes of course, followed
by *funny how things work out
that way,* my mind was
in quiet retreat. Where I
come from, bad things,
like secrets, held their breath
and hid behind wild privet hedges
and bowls of fruit, behind
Judy Garland albums and
Joni and tacos and
tubes of *Ban de Soleil,*
greasy and orange.

Child Psychologist

In 1965 or '66
when I was about nine
I decided that I wanted to be
a child psychologist.
I didn't know
that this was what I wanted to be
until one day
some neighborhood father
asked me
and out it came,
"child psychologist"
surprising even to me
but it made sense
as my mother had taken me
to see one once, a man
who let me sit at a low table
and play with small, life-like dolls.
I would arrange them into groups
and then he would ask me
to tell him about them
his voice patient
watching as I moved
the mother doll close to me,
the father doll far away,
the little boy doll
resting in the warmth
of the mid-day sun.

Skunk Cabbage

Back then, everyone's parents smoked. We even had a game we played, cigarette tag, where you'd have to shout out a brand of cigarettes before whomever was "it" could tag you. It's hard to imagine now, a group of children running around in the fading purple light of a summer evening with Marlboro! Winston! and Lucky Strike! erupting from their little mouths like it was normal, like everything was fine.

In the fall my brother and I would find chestnuts in the yard by side of our house near the woods, a part of the yard there was no reason to visit except for the chestnuts hiding in the shady grass. We would squat down and hold them in our hands, one at a time, feeling the dark shiny smoothness, like waxed wood.

I was taken to New York City for the first time in the winter to ice skate at Rockefeller Center and I remember seeing men on Fifth Avenue with charcoal braziers roasting chestnuts, the same sort of chestnuts that we found in our yard, but now warm and ready to eat. No one ever told us they were food.

In the spring the woods across the street from our house smelled of skunk cabbage, its pale green leaves sprouting out of the marshy soil while we played hide-and-seek. Once, I slipped and fell into a muddy creek soiling my clothes and when I got home I lied and told my mother that a girl I was playing with pushed me. I would like to talk to that girl, maybe bring her some spring flowers, tell her what it's been like living with lies, the damage done, the hunger.

Irish Twins

We aren't Irish
but every year
for a week
five days to be exact
we're the same age
a fact my brother
always took an avid delight
in reminding me
since his birthday came first
and for a little while
we were equals
simply brothers
getting along
not fighting
somehow able to take a break
from resentment
and rage
and it seemed
that even our parents
stopped fighting
and tensions ebbed
as our mother
made two cakes
threw two parties
but that was a long time ago
until this year
when I sent my brother a happy birthday text
not sure where
or in what condition
it would find him
or if he would respond
or even read it

but he wrote back
almost immediately
we're the same age for a week
and I smiled
although without any emojis
it felt serious
and I knew
that he was trying to bring back
that week
trying to give us again
those five days
when
for a brief while
everything was ok.

Lament

No one slept. The kitchen was empty.
Leaves gathered at the back door and no one knew
where the dog was or even thought about him.
Even the early morning light
was too much for the people there.
Passing clouds carried laments that echoed
in every room, floor to ceiling.

Elegy

When I talk about you I always say "my father" never "dad" and when people ask me *what did your dad do* or *when did your dad die*, I want to correct them, but I don't.

When your wife called and told me you were "gone" collapsed in your study, suddenly and without warning, my grief, the purity of it, took me by surprise.

Can you believe I think about you every day? The way I feel inside myself so much of the time, quiet and heavy, is how I think you felt too.

Once, when my career fell apart, you were the only one who understood, who had real sympathy.

It used to give me a secret, slightly vindictive thrill that my dog never warmed up to you the way most dogs did, the way you wanted him to. It was as if he somehow knew that I didn't want it, knew I couldn't tolerate it, watching you pet him, play with him.

I wish you hadn't been so loud.

I've been in therapy for decades and one of the saddest things I've ever had to feel is that moment when I was eleven and you took my brother and me for a walk to tell us that you were leaving, moving to California, and I couldn't feel it until I was nearly fifty.

I remember opening the gift you sent me for my high school graduation, a soft, leather toiletry bag and a bottle of cologne, things you thought a young man would need when he went off to college. I had that toiletry bag until well into my thirties.

You never really apologized except once when you'd been drinking you said *I did the best I could*. I believed you.

I admit that when I would visit you I looked forward to your drinking because it was the only time you would talk, could talk. I enjoyed drinking with you.

When I called you to tell you that I had HIV I was so nervous. I remember sitting on my bed, holding the phone to my ear, hearing your concern, your sadness.

When I had my first migraine at eight I was lying on the living room sofa, crying, thinking there was something wrong with my eyes, the pain was so great. You peered into my eyes to see if something was there, your voice worried but reassuring. It would've been a good time to tell you me you loved me.

I always liked your friends.

I miss your things. I want to go to your house and see your stuff, your handmade shoji screens, koa wood tables and Inuit art. I want to stand in your study and breathe and not feel nervous or afraid.

Sometimes I imagine you standing in mine, watching me work.

Remember we went camping once, took a road trip, just the two of us? I must have been fifteen. We made our way up the Pacific Coast Highway in your silver Chevy, stopping at campsites along the way until we got to Crater Lake. We'd never been alone together before and were so unused to each other's presence that sometimes we would go for what seemed like hours without talking.

Neither of us could believe how deep the water was, or how blue, like cobalt.

Jocks

When my father and I had the "Dad, you know I'm gay"
conversation he slowly leaned his heavy ex-football
player frame back into his black leather lounge chair,
cocked his head to one side and after swilling yet
another mouthful of scotch said, "you know, if I hadn't
gone to boarding school I probably would've been gay
too." It was late and we were alone in his bachelor executive
apartment. The languid southern California night air seeped
in through the sliding screen door inviting conversation
and confession and suddenly we were equals.
Decades later at his 75th birthday, the big guy, now shrunken
and limping but still moving forward like a linebacker,
introduces me to his old fraternity brothers and I can tell
by that certain glint in their eyes that they were
once in love with him.

My Psychiatrist Keeps Reminding Me That Depression is Anger Turned Inward

I've got this bell,
a kind of wind chime
that hangs on
the branch of an oak tree
outside my house.
It was a gift
I once gave
to my father,
a housewarming gift,
and after he died
his wife wanted
me to have it
so I took it
and hung it there
on that tree.
Sometimes
when the wind blows
and the bell rings
I think of him,
often imagining
that when he heard it ring
on some blustery day
he stopped
whatever he was doing
or was about to do
and thought of me—
but if I am honest
I doubt that he ever did,
I am pretty sure
this never happened
so that with each
wind-driven intonation
I am reminded
of how it's always been,

how I have always
only imagined
the tender moment,
his gesture of affection,
even trying to find it
in the sound of a bell.

Career Development

What were you doing that morning
catching the downtown #1 train at 5:45
listening to John Coltrane and Dollar Brand
and Aretha's gospel album
on your Walkman
for inspiration
spiritual sustenance
knowing only
that you were going to work
hardly believing that you got this job
at a methadone clinic
some kid from the suburbs
in a Kelly-green sweater
getting off at 23rd street
and walking east
towards the soon to be rising sun.
I can still see you
seated at a grey metal desk
by the window
of that storefront clinic
about to see your first clients
like the Italian girl from Staten Island
who brought you a box of chocolates
probably stolen
wishing you well
her eyes catching yours
or the aging lesbian from Hell's Kitchen
who was always high
about to nod off
who leans in close and tells you
that she's a *bull-dagger*
a term you'd never heard before
and all the while
you were excited
firmly believing

that this job was more than a career
was more than something
you were simply choosing to do.
But if only you'd listened closely
in the relative calm
of that urban predawn hour
you would have heard the echo
of your mother's screaming
in the middle of the night
this time like all the other times
desperate
shattering
out of control
her voice filling a house
where no one slept
where you believed no one was listening
but you
a boy of eight
who sat on the floor of the den in that house
next to the fireplace
still in his pajamas
holding in his hands
his mother's copy
of E. E. Cummings' *1x1*
that he found on the bookshelf
carefully turning the pages
staring at them
each one
calling him.

Fifty Minutes

What a curious thing it is to have made a living out of listening,
the ear attuned to the slightest pause, the vocal tremor,
the eye to any faint facial tic or quiver of a lip
to tell you of some untapped current

hour after hour so that it feels almost
devotional, this unearthing of words and truths
that rest in the air between you, where everything
comes from the inside out.

Sometimes it starts with a barrage of words,
other times with silence perhaps followed by
a stutter, but either way the room becomes full
as the hour breathes its own rhythm and the thing is

you never know what is going to happen next,
what story you are about to hear, what it is that
someone will bear to tell you in an office hushed,
muted and sufficiently insulated, a sanctuary, not only

for the one doing the telling, but for you too, the one
being told, for where else, except for maybe
the confessional box, does such a thing occur,
but yours is not the power to forgive or absolve

but only to receive, it is weight to be borne,
carried across thresholds and around hidden
corners until there is some glimpse of light
where, speaking in a whisper, you recount

the exact moment you were abandoned,
as if an entire adulthood never happened
and you were alone, only to find yourself
here, now, together.

Runaway Dorothy Was the Name of the Band

In the whirling dervish of time that is New York on a Friday
evening at dusk we run down the subway stairs to catch the

train that is just pulling into the station and as my foot
lands on the last step I hear the sound of a banjo being

played by a bluegrass band on the platform and I must
not cry as I jump into the car, the glare of the lights

making everyone's face look sterile, like we are riding
in a medicine cabinet, and I try to speak, to explain what

just happened but it doesn't come out right except to
comment on the exquisite juxtaposition of the music

and the setting but what I couldn't convey was an
Appalachian horizon, vast and deep, the hoe in the soil,

the laundry on the line, or the church pew with the
Methodist hymnal that had my mother's name inside,

a name she doesn't use anymore, but she stills knows
the hymns and can sing them, in harmony, and when

she does she is a country girl who can recite
the fifty-five counties of West Virginia in less than

thirty-seconds flat, something my brother and I used
to beg her to do, and we would all sing the state song

as we crossed the border on the old Route 60 but now
that girl is past eighty and what will I do when it is

all gone?

Playlist in June

Somewhere between Laura Nyro
and Leonard Cohen I decide to add
Burt Bacharach to the playlist I am making
the first few notes of Dusty Springfield's voice
singing *What the World Needs Now* bounce around
the airy room - living room dining room and kitchen
all in one - and can be heard outside by the pool
which is being heated because the nights are still chilly
and cannot be heard by our old dog who is fast asleep
on the rug by the fireplace having given up hope
for a ride in the Jeep his favorite thing
and then there you are standing next to me with
your food-stained blue cooking apron on and your even bluer eyes
and here we are carrying on waiting for houseguests to arrive
so I wonder what I will play next and I think
perhaps Jimmy Webb might be right his voice plaintive
and unadorned singing *Wichita Lineman* the song he wrote
I need you more than want you and I want you
for all time yes that should do the trick
hold everything together and be soft enough to
not wake the dog.

I watch him, my husband

I watch him, my husband
as he rides his bike in front of me on our way to the beach,
notice how his knees splay out just a bit,
his ankles turn in just a hair,
how his shoulders are relaxed as he steadily pedals
along in a way that seems so effortless, so easy,
and I realize that I am getting to see him as a boy—
that he has always ridden a bike exactly like this
so I ask him about being a boy and riding bikes
and he tells me that he rode his bike to school every day with his friends,
a small fact I had never known
even after twenty-seven years of being together,
twenty-seven years after that first night
when the scent of his cologne
slid down the back of my throat
as we kissed on the street in the East Village
and I would say to my roommate that
I had just met the man I was going to marry
which was the word I used to mean forever
in that time when silence equaled death,
but who could have predicted, what crystal ball
could have foretold that we would be here,
in this new century, as husbands
with a house and a pile of junk mail, with a drawer
full of cufflinks and collar stays and a vase stuffed full with poppies,
or that we would have bike locks and helmets and bottles of water
and be riding past sand dunes and tidal flats
and deep into a beech forest stopping to watch
as the sky turns impossibly pink.

Super Aging

The article in the *Times*
said that in order to have
a healthy alert brain
to become what it called
a SuperAger
it is necessary
to work hard at something
on a regular basis
so I thought about
all the things I do
that are hard
like Saturday's puzzle
like hot yoga
three times a week
which is really hard
and Pilates
and writing poems
and I was pleased
it seemed like enough
like I wasn't shirking my responsibility
to my brain
but then I thought
it's my heart that works the hardest
staying open as it does
to keeping me alive
faithfully prodding my brain
to counter
what psychiatrists call
intrusive thoughts
ones that occur without warning
thoughts where I wish I weren't here
like where I see myself
"accidentally" drowned
at the bottom of my pool
one gulp of water is all it would take

I'll think
while swimming laps alone
on a summer morning
and it's my heart that gets me
to the shallow end
where I will stand
remove my goggles
and notice perhaps
all the bees hovering
in the flowering crepe myrtle trees
or those thoughts of dying
of a deadly disease
that only these pills I take
prevent me from having
pills I sometimes think
I will simply stop taking
it would be so easy
but my heart phones in for refills
and sits me down again
here at this desk to write
so I wonder if it counts
to an aging brain
this hard work
of a devoted heart
this daily prompting
to live
this successful reminding
to always remember
not to forget
the secret joy
the humming of bees on a summer's day
their yellow bodies so sturdy
against those white blossoms.

In Traction

It is the first few weeks
of my retirement and
I am in physical therapy
where Tim is treating me first,
massaging me, telling me
about how his wife is French,
that he loves local history
and did I know that the empty lot
by the bridge in Sag Harbor
is going to become a small park
while he pushes up the sleeve of my shirt
to get at my shoulder
which has been in spasm ever since
I pinched a nerve in my neck
and is now in need
of his touch.
I am then delivered to Kris
who patiently guides me
through my exercises
speaking so softly
that I must ask him to repeat himself
with each new instruction
and as he does
I think of his family,
picturing a whole clan
of gentle, soft-spoken people,
allowing myself to imagine
what it must be like
to go through the world having been
raised that way, quietly.
Finally it's time for Laura
who puts me in traction
while telling me about her boyfriend
who got a job on a vineyard on the North Fork

and how he has to take two ferries
just to get there
which makes me think of my work,
all those years
of being a psychotherapist
and how I could walk to my office,
never leaving Greenwich Village
and usually taking my dog with me
who would sometimes be there
for six or seven clients
never moving except when someone cried,
curling up next to them
at their feet.
And now I am here,
in traction,
suspended, immobilized,
delivered even,
if only for fifteen minutes,
from the weight of wondering
what does one do with all the time
and from not knowing
what it means or how it will be
in this new place
amid all these new stories
and for the first time
to have only myself to help.

After being vaccinated, second dose, at Javits Convention Center, March 2021

Exhausted by fear
still wary of the subway
and tired of windy corners
and the unrelenting grid
I walk the High Line
home
from Hudson Yards to Greenwich Village.

At around 28th street
I come upon an elevated patch of grass
a field in miniature
strewn with snowdrops
and edged with crocuses.

All those people getting shots—
I wanted to cry
but I didn't know it until now
seeing these late winter flowers
standing here in front of this field
this scrap of earth
where life is carrying on
always
and everywhere
with or without us.

Birdbaths on Amazon

You tell me again that you want to buy a bird feeder
to hang outside our kitchen window
and again I object because of the mess with
all the shells on the ground and
those persistent determined squirrels
and besides they're not so pretty
and where exactly would we put it anyway
but I agree to go with you to the bird supply store
in Bridgehampton
the one I didn't want to go into last time
so I sat in the car
the one where I now discover
that the proprietor is so nice
with his booming friendly voice
a man who loves his store
a place chock full of bird paraphernalia
and who makes jokes
while he shows us the different kinds of feeders
some that squirrels can't get into
and you are loving it
kibitzing with him you would say
and laughing.
At the check-out counter
I see a guidebook about birds
Birding for Beginners
color coded
so you can find your bird
and I am reminded of my grandmother
who loved birds
who had such a book
and outside her kitchen window
was a bird feeder and a bird bath
oh Jay she would say
with her southern drawl

calling me out of the living room
when I was a little boy
sitting on the floor in front of the TV
watching Captain Kangaroo
come look at the cardinal!
and there we'd sit at the kitchen table
admiring the striking bird
her state's bird
so I decide to buy the book
because now I want the bird feeder
the squirrel proof one
and yes
we'll take those seeds too
the ones without shells
and then let's go home I say
to look at birdbaths on Amazon.
And in our dreams
aren't birds messengers of the gods
bringers of spirit
symbols of transcendence
I recall this from my days as a Jungian
a lifetime ago
but that was then
and this is now
where what matters most
is us and this home we have decided to make for ourselves
probably our last.

J **ay Kidd** has a Bachelor of Arts in Human Development and Social Relations from Earlham College and a Master of Divinity from Union Theological Seminary. For the past 40 years, he has worked in the field of mental health as a counselor, psychotherapist, life coach and HIV/AIDS educator. His poetry has appeared in many publications including *Bellevue Literary Review, Ruminate Magazine, The Florida Review, Atlanta Review, Crosswinds Poetry Journal, Vallum Magazine* and others. Jay is a past winner of *Ruminate Magazine*'s Janet B. McCabe Prize for Poetry as well as *Atlanta Review*'s International Poetry Competition. He is also a five-time Pushcart Prize nominee, and for the past 15 years, has studied the craft of writing at The Writers' Studio. Jay divides his time between New York City and East Hampton, New York, where he lives with his husband and dog.

Printed in the USA
CPSIA information can be obtained
at www.ICGtesting.com
JSHW082037191023
50523JS00008B/35